Proverbs for Teens

By
Jodi Green

All scripture quotations are from
The Believer's Study Bible: New King James
Version. 1991. Thomas Nelson, Inc. edited by W.A.
Criswell

INTRODUCTION

When I was in junior high school (middle school now days), I heard about Billy Graham's practice of reading five chapters of Psalms and one chapter of Proverbs every day. Since there are 150 chapters of Psalms and 31 chapters of Proverbs, that meant he read the entire books of Psalms and Proverbs every month. And since Psalms teaches us to relate to God, and Proverbs teaches us to relate to our culture, Billy Graham's idea seemed like a great one.

Dr. Graham's practice was to read the chapters of Proverbs according to the day of the month. For example, on the first day of the month he read Proverbs 1; the second day would be Proverbs 2, and so on. He read Psalms in order of the chapters, but we will discuss that more in the conclusion.

My hope for this book is to begin training you to read a chapter of Proverbs every day. Proverbs is a book of wisdom, and we all need a daily dose of Biblical wisdom. Reading only one verse of scripture per day is like eating one spoonful of cereal for breakfast. It is still good for you, but you need a whole bowl to be nourished physically. In the same way, one verse of scripture is good for you, but you need more if you are to grow spiritually.

The way to use this book is to keep it with your Bible, and read the chapter of Proverbs each day that corresponds with the day of the month. For example, if today is the 5th of the month, start with chapter 5 of Proverbs. Then read the devotion that goes with Day 5. I have chosen one verse in each chapter for you to think about for that day. The next month there will be a different verse to think about.

My prayer is that you will so fall in love with the daily reading of God's Word that you will grow to want more than a chapter a day. My goal is to eventually inspire you to read Psalms and Proverbs every day to encourage and train you in growing in favor with God and man.

Day 1 – Read Proverbs 1

"The fear of the Lord is the beginning of knowledge, but fools despise wisdom and instruction." (Verse 7)

So is there any such thing as a smart atheist? According to this verse, the answer is "no". If the fear ("awe") of the Lord is the beginning of knowledge, then a person who turns their back on God cannot be considered intelligent. They may appear to be smart in a worldly sense, but compared to eternity, the Bible calls them fools.

As a young person, you are continually bombarded by the message that earthly success is the most important goal. But you must remember this: it won't matter if you receive the highest awards this world can offer, if you have failed to honor God, you will have failed. Your goal must be to bring gold, silver and precious stones into eternity, rather than the wood, hay and stubble of a life caught up in worldly pursuits.

Day 2 - Read Proverbs 2

"For the Lord gives wisdom; from His mouth come knowledge and understanding." (Verse 6)

Most everyone would like to be smart. Young people are encouraged to study very hard for many years to gain the world's wisdom. Interesting studies have been done that show that the more highly educated a person becomes, the less likely that person is to believe God's Word is literally true.* God described this phenomenon in Romans 1:22, "Professing themselves to be wise, they became fools."

It is good to keep in mind during your years of schooling that only God gives wisdom, knowledge and understanding. It is not good to admire the false wisdom of this world and abandon seeking true wisdom. The false wisdom of the world wants to block out God and His Word, but we know the source of true wisdom.

* "One-Third of Americans Believe the Bible is Literally True" Gallup.com. May 25, 2007. Frank Newport

Day 3 – Read Proverbs 3

"Trust in the Lord with all your heart, and lean not on your own understanding." (Verse 5)

This is a very simple and straightforward statement, but it is one of the most difficult of God's commands for us to follow. We naturally want to lean on our own understanding. In fact, it is a defining characteristic of young people to look to their own understanding, dismissing the wisdom of their elders.

Our own understanding of life situations often fails us. But God will never fail. That is why the word is to trust Him, rather than ourselves. Throughout the book of Proverbs, God gives us repeated admonitions to trust God and to look to wise counsel from our elders. This does not come naturally. Our human nature, what the Bible refers to as the natural man, goes against God's principles. Only when we look to the Holy Spirit can we hope to trust God above our own hearts and minds.

Day 4 - Read Proverbs 4

"Wisdom is the principal thing; therefore, get wisdom. And in all your getting, get understanding."
(Verse 7)

During your teen years you spend a lot of time gaining knowledge. In fact, gaining knowledge is your main job in school. Unfortunately, most of the knowledge you gain during this time is worldly knowledge that will not last. Sometimes it may seem useless to spend so much time on something that is temporary.

But God's Word instructs you to "get wisdom"; and that "wisdom is the principal thing". Do you know the difference between wisdom and knowledge? Wisdom comes only from God. Proverbs continually shows us how to gain wisdom from God. Gaining knowledge may be your job in school, but it is temporary. Gaining a heart of wisdom will suit you for eternity.

Day 5 – Read Proverbs 5

"For the ways of man are before the eyes of the Lord, and He ponders all his paths." (Verse 21)

This is one of those chapters that might embarrass some teenagers because it is so graphic. But even though you may be surprised to find this picture of sex from a Biblical perspective, it is nonetheless Holy Spirit-inspired, and we learn much from it.

We learn that God knows and understands, and in fact created the human need and desire for sex. We also see the contrast between sexual sin and sexual purity. As in most of the chapters of Proverbs, God shows us the wise versus the foolish paths. Every person has the opportunity to choose their own path. We choose to follow God's way, or we choose to follow our own way. And either path we choose has consequences, as Proverbs reminds us repeatedly.

Day 6 - Read Proverbs 6

"For the commandment is a lamp, and the law a light; reproofs of instruction are the way of life." (Verse 23)

I can't think of any teenager that I know now, or ever have known (including myself), who enjoys having the rules and restrictions necessary to produce a Godly life. That's why the parallels of the wise and foolish are repeated so often in Proverbs. God knew it would be difficult in our flesh to be obedient to His Word. But He wants to show us all how much better it will be for us when we follow His ways. In Matthew, the path is "broad and easy that leads to destruction", and "hard and narrow that leads to life". The same idea is presented over and over in Proverbs.

If you could learn while you are young that His laws and commandments are a light to guide us on our path, you would save yourself so much trouble and heartache.

Day 7 – Read Proverbs 7

"For at the window of my house I looked through my lattice and saw among the simple; I perceived among the youths a young man devoid of understanding..." (Verses 6-7)

There are several things to notice about these verses. The first one is, how did the writer know that the young man was "devoid of understanding"? The answer is in the next verse: because of where he was going. The young man was foolish because he deliberately walked toward temptation, rather than avoiding it. Sometimes temptations sneak up on us, but often we are able to recognize where sin lies and choose to walk away.

God will put people in your life who can warn you when you are about to go the wrong way. But you must choose to listen to those warnings, sometimes even seek them out. You may even be the person in the position of warning someone else of the wrong path.

Day 8 – Read Proverbs 8

"Counsel is Mine, and sound wisdom; I am understanding; I have strength." (Verse 14)

When you read chapter 8, you recognize that the entire chapter is about the excellence of wisdom. In fact, since wisdom is an attribute (characteristic) of God, this chapter teaches us about God's character.

This particular verse shows us that all we have to do when we don't know what to do is to look to God's wisdom. And all we have to do when we feel weak is to lean on God's strength. Most of the time when we are really struggling with a decision, it is because we are not willing to commit to God's way. What we usually want is for God to bless the way we want to go rather than choose to go the way He shows us in His Word.

Day 9 – Read Proverbs 9

"Do not correct a scoffer, lest he hate you;
rebuke a wise man, and he will love you." (Verse 8)

There are at least two ways to look at this verse.
The first way is to consider whether you are a
scoffer or wise man (or woman!). According to
this verse, as well as many others in Proverbs, you
can determine this by how you respond to
correction. When someone corrects or rebukes
you, do you become angry and defensive of your
actions or words? Or do you use correction from
others as an opportunity to examine your
spiritually weak areas (which we all have!)?

The second way to look at this verse is to consider
whether you are mature enough in your faith to
recognize who would wisely welcome correction,
and whether you are able to offer correction with
grace and wisdom from above.

Day 10 – Read Proverbs 10

"He who gathers in summer is a wise son; he who sleeps in harvest is a son who causes shame." (Verse 5)

You probably do not live on a farm, and you may not even be considering farming as your potential life's work. So, would we skip over a Biblical truth if we thought it did not apply to us? Perhaps a better strategy would be to figure out if the truth presented actually does apply.

Even if you do not live on a farm, you still have responsibilities that need to be done at certain times. Only the very youngest children are free from responsibility and expectation. This verse is admonishing us to do our work at the proper time, rather than bringing shame to ourselves and our families by shirking responsibility.

In today's technology-filled world, there are so many ways for teens to fill their time. Be wise with your time and priorities.

Day 11 – Read Proverbs 11

"Where there is no counsel, the people fall; but in the multitude of counselors there is safety." (Verse 14)

So, the question here is, "Who should my counselors be?" As usual, the Bible provides our answer.

Since most of Proverbs is attributed to Solomon, we might assume this advice is from him. You might recall that Solomon's own son, Rehoboam listened to the wrong counselors and literally tore apart the kingdom of Israel. 1 Kings 12 is the account of how Rehoboam rejected the counsel of his elders and followed the counsel of the young men with whom he had grown up. The results were disastrous, both for him personally and for the nation of Israel.

There will always be voices around you trying to convince you to do this or that. If you are wise, you will seek wise counsel, and you will learn the difference between the wise and the foolish.

Day 12 – Read Proverbs 12

"The righteous should choose his friends carefully, for the way of the wicked leads them astray." (Verse 26)

As you may have noticed by now, God puts amazing emphasis in Proverbs on the type of friends we have. He also provides in this book many ways to recognize wise and foolish companions.

A wise young person will heed their parents' warnings of wise and foolish friends. Many times your parents will recognize traits that will have unpleasant consequences before you do. Learn to seek their advice about the people you spend the most time with.

Realize also that Jesus was a "Friend of sinners". And he admonished us not to judge others in a condemning way. So, even though you must choose friends carefully, we must also build bridges to share the gospel and encourage the foolish to seek Christ.

Day 13 - Read Proverbs 13

"He who guards his mouth preserves his life, but he who opens wide his lips shall have destruction." (Verse 3)

We have all heard the warning to "Think before you speak," and this verse gives the consequences for not guarding our mouths.

This is another Proverb that should be thought of in at least two ways. The first is the discipline of words. We have all said things we did not mean to say, or wished we had not said. No one is born with the ability to control their tongue. We must all learn self-control in this area. You will find all through the Bible ways to learn the words that are pleasing to God.

But since this verse does not specifically identify spoken words, we might also consider guarding what goes into our mouths. Other Proverbs speak more specifically about gluttony, but think about the ways that what we feed our bodies can be destructive as well.

Day 14 – Read Proverbs 14

"There is a way that seems right to a man, but its end is the way of death." (Verse 12)

Notice that the writer does not say, "There is a way that seems right to a fool…" He is showing us that even a good man can be misled, and it may even seem to be a good way. Many times, especially for those earnestly seeking the Lord, Satan will tempt with a counterfeit good rather than something obviously bad. There are many potential side streets for Christians that may seem good, but are not God's best way.

Thankfully God does not try to make His way difficult to find. He did say His way would be difficult to follow (Matthew 7:14), but not difficult to find. In fact, Proverbs is full of instructions for finding God's way.

It is not often difficult to decide between good and evil. But deciding between good and best can only be done in the power of the Holy Spirit and careful study of His Word.

Day 15 – Read Proverbs 15

"The ear that hears the rebukes of life will abide among the wise." (Verse 31)

So what exactly are "the rebukes of life" and why do they matter? A rebuke is simply a form of correction. The "rebukes of life" are going to come in many different ways for you. The first and most obvious are the rebukes from your parents. Your parents' rebukes are meant to protect you from dangerous error. If you can learn to listen to their correction in your life, you will be among the wise. All of us can think of teenagers who ignored their parents' warnings and ended foolishly, and sometimes permanently.

Hearing the rebukes of life suggests that it is neither necessary nor wise to learn everything the hard way. The rebukes of life are not always pleasant, but the lessons learned and the tragedies prevented will put you in the place of the wise.

Day 16 – Read Proverbs 16

"There is a way that seems right to a man, but its end is the way of death." (Verse 25)

You do not need to turn back to Day 14 to see that this is the exact same verse repeated two chapters later. Now if the exact same words appear twice in two chapters, or even in the whole Bible, we might correctly surmise that these words deserve special consideration.

To further discuss this important truth, we might think about the fact that, most of the time, what seems right to me is what pleases my selfish, sinful self at any given moment. God's will is almost always the exact opposite of what I would naturally choose. That is why we are instructed to walk by faith, not by sight (2 Corinthians 5:7). So, when you consider what seems right to you, you must first be sure that what you really want is what God wants. If you do not want what God wants, your heart probably does not belong to Him. Be sure that you have decided to walk in His ways eternally.

Day 17 – Read Proverbs 17

"Rebuke is more effective for a wise man than a hundred blows on a fool." (Verse 10)

Even though Jesus taught us that we must not call someone a fool (Matthew 5:22), Proverbs clearly warns us to recognize the qualities of a fool. All through this book, God gives us descriptions that show exactly what makes a person a fool.

In this particular verse, the defining characteristic is not responding to correction or discipline. Is this theme beginning to sound familiar? Again, any message that is repeated throughout scripture is worth carefully considering how it applies to our own life situations.

So again, how do you respond to correction? Do you use rebuke and correction to learn, or do you become defensive and angry? No one likes discipline, but we all must endure it to grow and mature in Christ.

Day 18 – Read Proverbs 18

"Death and life are in the power of the tongue, and those who love it will eat its fruit." (Verse 21)

This is a rather dramatic statement about the impact of our words. Proverbs seems to want to show that the power of what we say cannot be over-exaggerated.

All of us are impacted by the words that are spoken to us, as well as the words that we ourselves speak. Every person has been both encouraged and devastated by the words from another person's mouth. And we have all seen others lifted up or hurt because of words we have spoken. We have very little control over the words that are spoken to us, but we have absolute control over the words we speak.

What does "those who love it will eat its fruit" mean? Is "it" here the tongue or the power of the tongue? Probably both. And the consequences are life or death to the hearer.

Day 19 – Read Proverbs 19

"There are many plans in a man's heart, nevertheless the Lord's counsel – that will stand." (Verse 21)

How do you know when your decisions are from your own heart or from the Lord's counsel? How do you know if the Lord spoke to you on a matter, or you just want something so much?

Notice this verse does not tell us not to make plans. But God does show us plainly that many of our own plans are not God's plans for us. To learn to listen to the voice of God above the clamor of the world and above our own heart is the single greatest discipline we can learn. We can only learn to discern God's voice by learning His Word, consciously being willing to turn away from the world's allure and the selfishness in our own hearts.

The world screams at us every day in a multitude of ways; the Lord whispers to us from His Word. Learn to listen to Him.

Day 20 – Read Proverbs 20

"It is honorable for a man to stop striving, since any fool can start a quarrel." (Verse 3)

Perhaps there is nothing more to say about this verse. Read it again. Since it is such a simple and direct observation, why is it so difficult to follow?

First notice that this verse refers to honor for a man. It does not say "boy". So plainly it is a mark of maturity to be able to stop striving. The comparison is first between maturity and immaturity. Then in the second part of the verse the comparison is wise to foolish.

Whom do you strive with? Who are you most likely to start a quarrel with? If you have siblings, that might be your first battleground. Do all these Biblical admonitions relate to family relationships? Absolutely they do. And what about striving with your parents, teachers or others in authority over you? The mature and wise young person stops striving.

Day 21 – Read Proverbs 21

"A man who wanders from the way of understanding will rest in the assembly of the dead." (Verse 16)

When your heart and mind are tender towards God and His Word, you can feel immediately when you wander even one step from "the way of understanding." You sense almost instantly when you are not pleasing God in your thoughts, words or actions. It is possible to develop the habit of wandering from the ways of God so often that you do not notice you are doing it. The Bible refers to this as a "seared conscience" (1 Timothy 4:2).

But it is also possible to remain on the path of understanding, keeping your heart and mind trained on the ways of God. The most obvious way to stay on that path is to spend daily time in God's Word.

Day 22 - Read Proverbs 22

"A good name is to be chosen rather than great riches, loving favor rather than silver and gold." (Verse 1)

You may have noticed the emphasis in Proverbs on your reputation. Basically every chapter has something to say about what others see in us. This verse says you should choose a good reputation above anything on earth. Riches and gold are mentioned since that is what most people strive for in their lives.

So what is a good name? What comes to your mind when you hear names like Adolf Hitler, Judas Iscariot, Osama bin Laden, or Cain? Now what do you think of when you hear John the Baptist, Billy Graham, C.S. Lewis, or Jesus? What do people think of when they hear your name? Do they think of Godly character, the fruit of the Spirit (like love or self-control?), or something not so good? How we present ourselves to others is important to God. And pleasing God is better than great riches.

Day 23 – Read Proverbs 23

"They have struck me but I was not hurt; they have beaten me but I did not feel it. When shall I awake, that I may seek another drink?" (Verse 35)

This verse describes the mind-numbing effects of sinning against God. Modern society calls this addiction. The Bible calls it sin. The effect of continual sin is that the sinner numbs himself (or herself) to the consequences of that sin, no matter how painful. The particular sin noted in this verse is alcoholism. Interestingly, the Bible never implies that these types of sins are simply diseases that some people have and some don't. Instead, all such addictions (gluttony, sexual sin, alcoholism, anger, etc.) are included in lists of particular sins God hates.

The reason for God's hatred of particular sins is clear. The more we repeat a particular sin, the easier it becomes to do it again. Then our hearts harden against doing God's will. To keep our hearts soft toward God is the goal.

Day 24 – Read Proverbs 24

"Do not rejoice when your enemy falls, and do not let your heart be glad when he stumbles; lest the Lord see it and it displease Him, and He turn away His wrath from him." (Verses 17-18)

Proverbs provides many specific instructions about what to do in particular situations. Proverbs teaches us not only what to do, but also how to think, or what attitudes we should have. This one is a particular challenge for all of us. In our fallen human state, we cannot help but be glad when someone who has wronged us gets what they deserve.

Sometimes we mock openly when our enemies have trouble, but these verses refer to the attitude of our hearts that no one sees except God. Verse 18 says that God may even change your enemy's circumstances for good based on the attitude of your heart. That should be a sobering thought about the importance of our thoughts and attitudes before a Holy God.

Day 25 – Read Proverbs 25

"Whoever has no rule over his own spirit is like a city broken down, without walls." (Verse 28)

God's Word clearly instructs us to have control over our impulses and desires. Any time we make excuses for disobedience ("I was tired," "I forgot," "I wasn't thinking," "I didn't know," etc.) we are refusing to accept responsibility to control our thoughts, actions or words.

Reading Proverbs every day teaches us so many ways to practice self-control. Self-control is learned gradually as we mature. For example, most parents do not expect the same level of self-control from a five year old as they would from a fifteen year old. When you hear, "You are acting like a two year old," you are not being complimented on your self-control, since a two year old has not yet matured in that area.

If the Holy Spirit lives in you, He is producing His fruit in you, which includes self-control. (See Galatians 5:22-23)

Day 26 – Read Proverbs 26

"Do you see a man wise in his own eyes? There is more hope for a fool than for him." (Verse 12)

Keep in mind that Solomon, the wisest man in history, is the presumed writer here. So, even a person esteemed as wise cautions us against believing ourselves to be wise. We must continue to keep in our minds that God is the source of all wisdom. In fact, a person who does not acknowledge the Source of wisdom is pronounced a fool (see Psalm 14:1).

You will be tempted often to believe yourself to be wise. Sometimes you will believe with all your heart that you know better than perhaps the person to whom God has given decision-making power over you (parents, teachers, coaches, speed limit laws, etc.). But you will be wise to respectfully acknowledge the Source of wisdom, and be sure that your actions are in line with His Word.

Day 27 – Read Proverbs 27

"As iron sharpens iron, so a man sharpens the countenance of his friend." (Verse 17)

Again and again in Proverbs we see the importance of choosing friends wisely. At every stage of life it is urgent to develop friendships that will sharpen rather than dull you.

This can be applied in at least two ways. The first and most obvious is to have some friends who are more mature than you, both spiritually and mentally. These friends will probably be older than you, and you can think of these friends as mentors. In order to be sharpened you will have to spend time with them.

The second application is to be the sharpener for someone else. This can be your friend who is seeking after God, or it can be someone less mature in faith. Your sharpening should always have a positive effect on the countenance of your friend.

Day 28 – Read Proverbs 28

"He who trusts in his own heart is a fool, but whoever walks wisely will be delivered." (Verse 26)

In His divine wisdom, God gives us many ways to consider the importance of not leaning on our own understanding (see Proverbs 3:5). So what exactly does it mean to trust our own heart? What does it mean to walk wisely? From what will you be delivered?

If you have read the chapters of Proverbs so far, your mind may go back to the qualities of the wise and the foolish. God's Word tells us plainly what it means to walk wisely. So, obviously the first step in walking wisely is to study what God has to say about it. The more we read God's Word, the less we trust our own heart.

You might want to keep a notebook to write specific ways to walk wisely from God's Word.

Day 29 – Read Proverbs 29

"The fear of man brings a snare, but whoever trusts in the Lord shall be safe." (Verse 25)

If we could all learn not to be afraid of what others think of us, we would all be better off. In fact, this verse uses the word "safe" for trusting God's opinion over anyone else's. What would we be safe from if we trusted God and not man? A "snare" is a trap or something bad that we cannot escape from. Living our lives in fear of what others think brings trouble in at least two ways.

The first snare is that you can never please all of the people all of the time. So, to be afraid of others' opinion of you puts you in a frustrating trap. It can also put you in a dangerous trap if the people you are afraid of are evil. The second snare is that only God's opinions are reliable and true. So, to live to please God rather than other people brings peace and safety.

Day 30 – Read Proverbs 30

"Do not add to His words, lest He rebuke you and you be found to be a liar." (Verse 6)

Of course, this is God speaking directly about the completeness of His Word. There are two ways to consider how you might be adding to God's Word. The first one is how to know if you are adding to His words. The most obvious answer to this one is that you must study His Word daily to see and understand exactly what it does say. As I have emphasized repeatedly, reading God's Word daily is the only way to obedience to Him.

The second way to consider this verse has to do with what you think God may be telling you to do in a certain situation. According to this verse, you must find everything you think God is telling you in His Word. You must not say, "God told me such and such" if you did not find it in His Word. You may feel God leading you in a certain direction at times, but you must always consider how easily deceived we are and look only to Him.

Day 31 – Read Proverbs 31

"Charm is deceitful and beauty is passing, but a woman who fears the Lord, she shall be praised." (Verse 30)

Modern youth culture judges a young woman on outward appearances. According to this verse, we might assume this has been happening since ancient times. It is natural to be attracted to someone based on looks alone, especially when you are young. But, as usual, God wants to shift our focus away from earthly, temporary values and focus on Godly, eternal values.

This truth is emphasized many times in the Bible (1 Samuel 16:7, 1 Peter 3:3-4, and others). No matter what age you are, it is difficult not to admire someone simply for their outer beauty. But this verse reminds us that outward beauty passes as we age. Only a woman who fears the Lord will ultimately have value.

Be careful not to be caught up with earthly, temporary things. Focus on the eternal things.

CONCLUSION

I hope reading through the book of Proverbs has inspired you and brought you closer to God. I hope if you did not make it to your Bible reading every day, that you will keep trying. Don't give up if you miss a day or even several days. Just pick back up where you left off; believe me, God is still there waiting to shower you with the blessings of His Word.

There will be more books in this series. If you would like to continue on your own, keep reading Proverbs every day according to the date. Then add a chapter of Psalms in the same way. You can begin Psalms by reading the chapter that corresponds with the calendar date as well. Then, each month you can either read the same chapters, or simply add 30 to the chapter you are reading. For example, on the 5th of the month, you would read Psalm 5 and Psalm 35; on the 6th, you would read Psalm 6 and Psalm 36. The next month you would add another 30 and read Psalm 5, Psalm 35 and Psalm 65. You would continue to add 30 until you are reading 5 Psalms in a day. It would look like this:

Day 1: Psalms 1, 31, 61, 91, 121
Day 2: Psalms 2, 32, 62, 92, 122
(and so on until the end of the month)

Another way is to simply read Psalms 1-5 on day one, 6-10 on day two, and so on. This was Dr. Graham's practice.

That may be more than you can do every day. But just read what you can. Some days you might have time to read all five Psalms and a Proverb, and some days you might be able to only read a few verses of one chapter. The point is not how many chapters you can read in a day. The point is to read something from God's Word every day. This particular plan is simply a guideline.

I have personally been blessed in my life to have begun reading Psalms and Proverbs most days since I was in junior high school. I hope you will find the same blessing from the daily reading of God's Word. To read and obey God's Word is the path of life.

Made in the USA
Lexington, KY
24 January 2017